Half-hitched Carrick Bend Knot

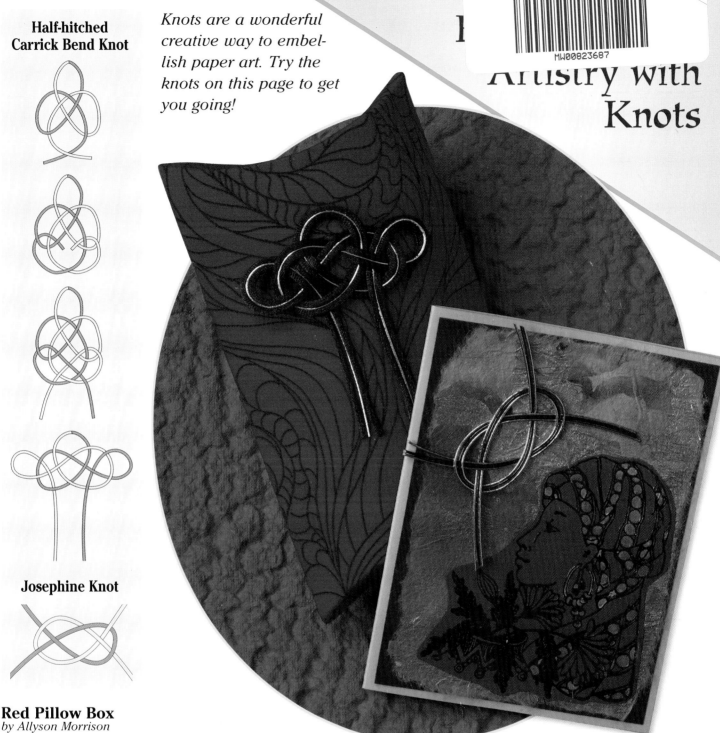

Knots are a wonderful creative way to embellish paper art. Try the knots on this page to get you going!

Josephine Knot

Red Pillow Box
by Allyson Morrison

MATERIALS: 8½" x 11" sheet Red cardstock • 8½" x 11" Piece Red patterned paper • Pillow box template or XL *Ellison* Letter Machine & die #B78403C for Box #3 • Two 18" lengths of 2mm Black satin rattail cord • 18" Silver Mizuhiki cord • Spray bottle of fabric stiffener • Pencil • Scissors • Clear tape • Glue stick

INSTRUCTIONS: Glue paper to cardstock with glue stick. If using template, place template on cardstock side of laminate. Trace outline on cardstock. Cut out pillow box, do not assemble. If using machine, place laminate against die with paper side touching cutting surface. Cut out pillow box with Box #3 die. If satin cord is too stiff to tie, rinse in water, remove, smooth out kinks. Tie knot while still damp, lay flat to dry. If knot shape does not hold, spray with stiffener, reshape and let dry. Following diagram, tie Half-hitched Carrick Bend knot using 2 strands of Black satin cord. Follow path of knot with 1 strand of Silver Mizuhiki cord to make triple strand knot. Place Silver cord between the Black strands. Trim knot ends. Glue to top of pillow box. Assemble using glue stick. Let dry.

Josephine Knot Card *by Allyson Morrison*

MATERIALS: Cardstock (5½" x 8½" Teal, 4" x 5¼" Black, 4" x 4" Brown) • 4½" x 6" piece *Printworks* Thailand Momigami paper • *Limited Edition* #18250 rubber stamp • Clear embossing ink • Black embossing powder • Heat gun • Four 18" strands Green Mizuhiki cord.• Two 18" strand of Black Mizuhiki cord • *Dove* Blender pen • *Pearl-Ex* powdered pigments (Super Copper, Brilliant Gold)
• *Powdered Pearls* powdered pigments (Plum, Turquoise) • Scissors • Glue

INSTRUCTIONS: Fold Teal cardstock in half. Tear edges of Momigami paper to form decorative edge. Glue to Black cardstock allowing rim of Black to show. Stamp image onto Brown cardstock with clear ink. Immediately dust with Black embossing powder and emboss with heat gun. Color image with powdered pigments and blender pen. Dip pen tip into pigment, color image, wipe pen tip clean, repeat with new color. Cut out completed image. Glue onto lower right of marbled Black cardstock. Glue decorated card onto Teal card front. Tie Josephine knot with Black cords following diagram. Adjust size so body of knot is 1¾" long. Follow path of knot on each side with Green cords to form a triple strand knot, Green, Black, Green. Trim ends. Glue knot in upper left of card.

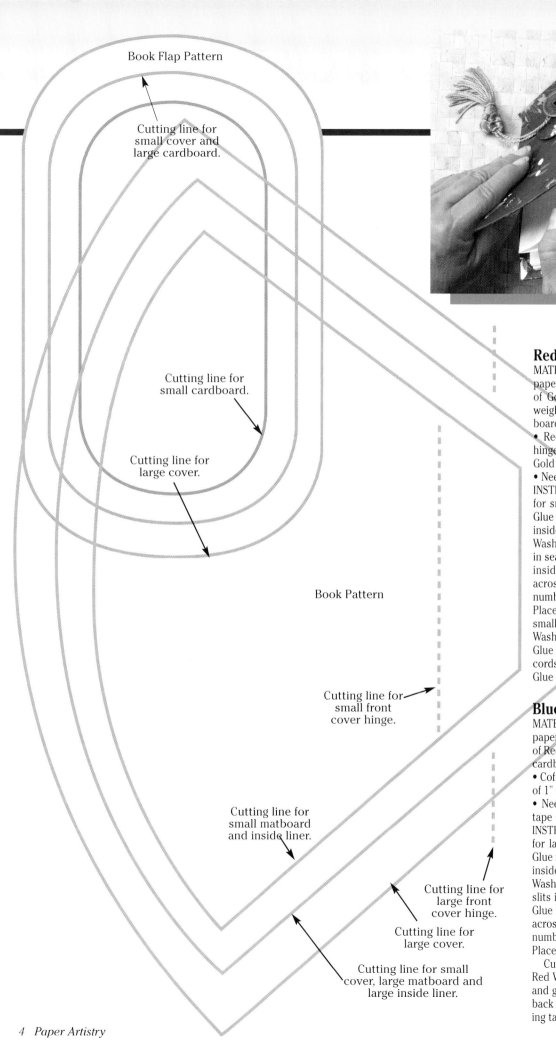

Book Flap Pattern

Cutting line for
small cover and
large cardboard.

Cutting line for
small cardboard.

Cutting line for
large cover.

Book Pattern

Cutting line for
small front
cover hinge.

Cutting line for
small matboard
and inside liner.

Cutting line for
large front
cover hinge.

Cutting line for
large cover.

Cutting line for small
cover, large matboard and
large inside liner.

Red Book

MATERIALS: Two 6" x 9" pieces of Red Washi paper • Two 5" x 8" pieces and one 3" x 5" piece of Gold Washi paper • 3" x 5" Piece of lightweight cardboard • Two 5" x 8" pieces of matboard • Small coffee filters • 2 Chinese coins • Red faceted acrylic stone • 4" of 1" Ribbon for hinge • 6" of ¼" Red sheer ribbon • 6" Fine Gold cord • 6" of Gold cord • Heavy duty thread • Needle • ¹⁄₁₆" Hole punch • Glue

INSTRUCTIONS: Using pattern, cut matboard for small book. Cut hinge from top cover only. Glue ribbon on back of matboard and hinge. Cut inside liners from Gold and covers from Red Washi paper. Glue covers to matboards, cut slits in seam allowances, fold to back and glue. Glue inside liners over raw edges. Punch holes across spine. For pages, punch holes in desired number of coffee filters to match holes in spine. Place pages in cover and sew to secure. Cut small flap from cardboard, cover with Gold Washi paper. Cut slits in edge, fold to back, glue. Glue flap around spine. Tie coins on ribbon and cords. Glue ends of ribbon and cords on flap. Glue stone to cover ends.

Blue Book

MATERIALS: Two 7" x 10" pieces of Blue Washi paper • Two 6" x 9" pieces and one 4" x 6" piece of Red Washi paper • 3" x 5" piece of lightweight cardboard • Two 6" x 9" pieces of matboard • Coffee filters • Chinese coin • Gold tassel • 5" of 1" ribbon for hinge • Heavy duty thread • Needle • ¹⁄₁₆" hole punch • Foam mounting tape • Glue

INSTRUCTIONS: Using pattern, cut matboard for large book. Cut hinge from top cover only. Glue ribbon on back of matboard and hinge. Cut inside liners from Red and covers from Blue Washi paper. Glue covers on matboards, cut slits in seam allowances, fold to back and glue. Glue inside liners over raw edges. Punch holes across spine. For pages, punch holes in desired number of coffee filters to match holes in spine. Place pages in cover and sew to secure.

Cut large flap from cardboard and cover with Red Washi paper. Cut slits in edge, fold to back and glue. Glue flap around spine. Glue tassel on back of coin and attach coin to flap with mounting tape.

Coffee Filter Booklets

Coffee filters form the pages of these fan-shaped books accented with coins and fibers.

1. Trace pattern and cut out matboard for book. Score on dashed line.

2. Cover front and back of matboard with paper.

3. Punch holes across spine.

4. Punch holes in desired number of pages to match spine.

5. Place pages inside covers and sew book together. Glue flap to cover.

1. Score and fold front up and flap down.

2. Punch holes. Slip ends of cord through holes.

3 Fold paper strips. Glue first strip to right side of bag.

4. Glue second strip to left side of bag.

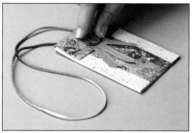

5. Glue trimmed ribbon and coin to flap.

Turn Outdated CDs into Works of Art.

Lilac Spirit Bag

MATERIALS: Decorative Yuzen paper (3" x 11" and 1½" x 9") • Lilac textured paper (3" x 11" and 1½" x 9") • Fusible webbing • Chinese coin • 12" of ⅜" Lilac grosgrain ribbon • 24" multi-colored rattail cord • ⅛" hole punch• Glue stick • White craft glue

INSTRUCTIONS: Fuse matching Yuzen and Lilac papers together. Place fusible web, web side down on back of one piece of Yuzen paper. With iron set at cotton, iron paper for 10 seconds to melt adhesive following manufacturer's instructions. When cool, remove backing paper and place Lilac paper right side up on web and apply hot iron to fuse 2 sheets together.

With pencil mark 1½" down from top on long side for flap fold. Fold bottom edge of strip up to pencil mark and crease bottom of bag. Front and back of bag will be 4¾". Fold flap over and crease. Open top flap and determine where yarn or cord will be attached on upper part of back and mark with pencil on inside of bag, punch holes 1" apart. Insert cord through holes, tie off inside bag. Fold 1½" x 9" strip in half lengthwise. Cut to make two 4½" strips. Wrap around and glue to side edges of bags to form side seams. Glue 3 short pieces of Lilac ribbon under coin on flap to make closure.

CD Shard Pin

MATERIALS: Pastel Pink and Green Yuzen paper scraps • CD • Butterfly charm • 12 glass beads (Pink, Green, Crystal) • Pin back • 3 Jump rings • 3 Eye pins • Metallic Gold paint pen • Matte acrylic medium • Long tweezers • Bone folder • Round-nose pliers • Heat gun • Hand drill • Sponge brush • White glue

INSTRUCTIONS: Using tweezers or pliers to hold CD, apply heat 2" from CD with heat gun moving back and forth on one side and following desired shape of pin for about 60 seconds. Cut desired shape from CD using regular scissors. The tweezers and CD will be hot, be careful. Try to keep plastic as flat as possible. If buckling occurs,

reheat and press under weight to flatten. The paper will be easier to smooth if plastic stays flat.

Apply glue in a thin even coat to one surface of CD and wrap with paper scrap slightly larger than shard, fold edges to back, smoothing paper with bone folder. Apply additional adhesive to edges and secure on back. Add paper scraps in a collage effect and make sure paper is glued down securely. When dry, seal with medium, let dry.

Drill 3 holes near bottom edge of covered piece. Attach 3 jump rings with pliers. Thread 3 or 4 beads on each eye pin, make a loop in straight end of pin with round-nose pliers and attach to jump rings. Glue on butterfly charm. Paint back of pin Metallic Gold and attach pin back.

Colorful CD Art & Folded Envelopes

by Lea Cioci

Turn CDs into wearable art and home decor accents. Present them in a matching bag or envelopment.

CD Ornament

MATERIALS: Red and Black script Yuzen paper • Lilac textured paper • Black cardstock • CD • *Inkadinkado* Asian calligraphy rubber stamp • Permanent Burgundy ink • 2 Red glass beads • 24 gauge Brass wire • Face charm • *Art Accents* Nippon postage paper collage element • Postage stamp decorative scissors • Craft drill • Tacky White glue

INSTRUCTIONS: Apply glue sparingly and use piece of Black script paper cut slightly larger to cover CD, folding edges over onto back side. Apply additional glue to edges if necessary to secure to back. Tear scraps of Red script Yuzen paper and glue randomly on Black paper. Stamp Asian calligraphy on torn Lilac paper, let dry. Glue in center of CD. Cut collage element from sheet of Nippon postage paper using Stamp scissors. Glue on CD as shown. Glue charm in place. If desired, cut a circle slightly smaller than CD from Black cardstock and glue to back of CD to cover decorative paper edges and finish back. To attach the beads, drill holes in CD. Thread beads on wire and through holes. Twist ends to secure.

Red & Black Envelope

MATERIALS: Two 5" x 14½" pieces of Black and Red Japanese script Yuzen paper • Two 2" x 6" and two 2" x 2" pieces of Red Japanese script Yuzen • Metallic Gold and Black cardstock • Two 2" x 6" pieces of copy paper • Fusible web • *Hero Arts* postoid rubber stamp • Black pigment ink • Gold embossing powder • Chinese coin replica • Brass charm • Asian good luck symbol punch • Red and Gold fibers • Black tassel • Heat gun • Postage stamp decorative scissors • Glue stick or paper adhesive • White glue

INSTRUCTIONS: Use fusible web to adhere 1 long piece of Red script Yuzen to 1 long piece Black Yuzen script paper. With pencil mark 2½" down from top on short side. This indicates flap fold. Fold bottom of strip up for bottom of envelope. Fold flap over and crease. Use copy paper and glue stick to line 6" strips of Red Yuzen, to prevent Black paper from showing through when Red paper is glued to it. Fold both lined Red script strips in half lengthwise. Glue on sides of envelope. Glue fibers and tassel to front of flap. Punch good luck symbol from Gold cardstock and back with Red paper and plain cardstock cut to fit. Glue over ends of fibers. Decorate front of envelope with small squares of Red script paper, attach Chinese coin and Brass charm. Stamp postoid on Black cardstock with Black ink. Emboss stamped image with Gold powder. Cut out with Stamp scissors, glue on front of envelope. Attach additional scraps of Red paper to back of envelope.

Spirit Bag & Envelope patterns on pages 8 & 9.

Beautiful Artistry Envelopes for CDs

Continued from page 7

These fabulous envelopes are just what is needed to send a note, an invitation, photo or card to that special someone.

Lilac Spirit Bag
Pattern

Fold

Fold

Valentine Card

Fold

Valentine Card
by Sally Traidman
MATERIALS: 5½" x 8½" piece of Pale Blue cardstock • 2¾" x 3¾" piece of Gold Washi paper • 3½" x 4" piece and ⅛" x 6" strip of flower print Washi paper • 2½" x 3½" piece of Lilac and 4" square of Metallic Gold paper • 6" of ½" Pale Blue ribbon • 1¼" heart punch • ⅛" circle punch • Brass heart charm • Toothpick • Glue
INSTRUCTIONS: Fold cardstock in half for card. Glue Lilac and Gold paper on card. Fold 3 corners of flower print to center to make an envelope. Glue bow and charm to secure envelope, glue on card. Punch out 3 Gold hearts and punch 2 holes in each. Thread ⅛" strip of paper through holes and curl ends with a toothpick. Glue the hearts on the envelope.

Fold

**Red and Black Envelope
Pattern**

Happy Holidays from Santa

Have you ever noticed how Christmas always seems to be just around the corner? Well, here are some ideas you can begin anytime!

Folded Santas can be used as tree ornaments, to embellish cards or attached to a package for decoration. You'll have no trouble making these happy guys, just follow the easy step-by-step folding diagrams!

Oh yes, the Santa ornament is a great way to use your left over beads.

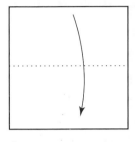

1. Fold paper in half.

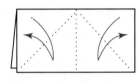

2. Fold rectangle in half, open. Crease along the dotted line.

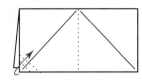

3. Fold corner in ⅛". Fold in again. On the back side, repeat on left corner only.

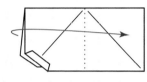

4. Fold rectangle in half.

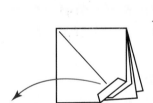

5. Open flap and press down.

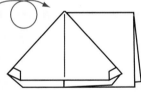

6. Turn over.

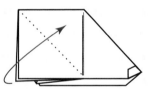

7. Fold up along the dotted line.

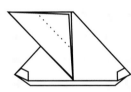

8. Crease top flap along the dotted line.

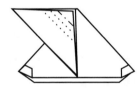

9. Crease and fold ⅛" above the first crease you made.

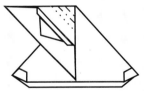

10. Fold over along the first crease.

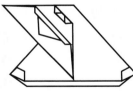

11. Fold opposite corner down toward the back. Fold forward along the dotted line.

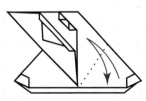

12. Fold side up along the dotted lines.

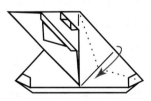

13. Crease along dotted lines, pull toward you and fold to flatten.

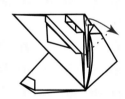

14. Fold to the side to make one arm.

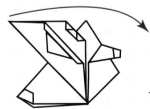

15. Bring entire flap over.

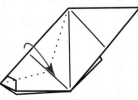

16. Crease along dotted lines and pull toward you.

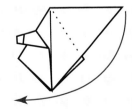

17. Wrap around and fold along the dotted line.

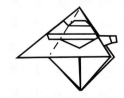

18. Fold this piece behind but not around the other arm.

19. Your Santa should look like the diagram.

Folded Paper
Santa Claus

alias - Saint Nick
aka - Kris Kringle

by Kathy Yoshida

Take time this year to prepare for the holidays. Include the whole family in making your decorations and holiday greeting cards. Set aside one evening a week for family night and use that time to get into the creative spirit of the holidays!

Share stories about past Christmases and wishes for the future. And don't forget to take plenty of snapshots for your scrapbook album. You can even make extra Santas to embellish your album pages!

Santa Folds   on page 10

Use one 6" square of double-sided Origami paper (or make a large ornament with an 11" x 11" square of paper, or any size square of paper)

Santa Ornament

MATERIALS: 6" square of Metallic Red/White paper • 4 Green glass beads • 2 Blue seed beads • 24 gauge Red wire • Round-nose pliers • Glue

INSTRUCTIONS: Fold Santa following diagrams. Insert 10" of wire through center of Santa. Thread glass beads on wire and spiral ends to secure beads.

Santa Card

MATERIALS: 6" square of Red/White paper • 4³⁄₄" x 5" Piece of Red cardstock • 4¹⁄₄" x 4¹⁄₂" piece of Red Washi paper • 3" x 4" Piece of Green handmade paper with torn edges • 4 Gold eyelets • 2 Blue seed beads • Eyelet setter • Hammer • Glue

INSTRUCTIONS: Attach Washi paper to cardstock with eyelets. Glue Green paper on Washi paper. Fold Santa following diagrams. Glue seed beads for eyes. Glue Santa on card.

Artfully Folded Flying Cranes

by Kathy Yoshida

Crane Folds

6" square of paper

Flying cranes flutter and flitter on this lovely jeweled mobile and elegant jeweled ornament. Make several mobiles varying the length and hang side by side to create a curtain. You'll love the way they look!

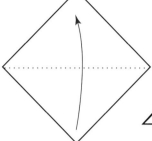

1. Turn square and fold into triangle.

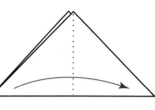

2 Fold triangle in half again.

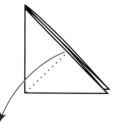

3. Open each pocket, flatten into square.

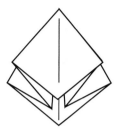

4. You paper should look like the diagram.

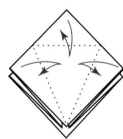

5 Crease along dotted lines as shown.

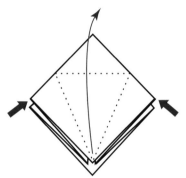

6. Pull flap up. As you pull, fold in side flaps using creased as a guide.

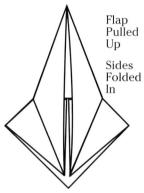

Flap Pulled Up

Sides Folded In

7. Your paper should look like the diagram.

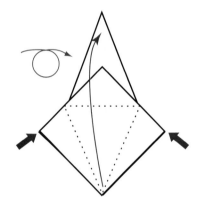

8. Repeat on other side.

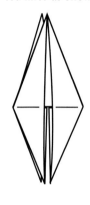

9. You paper should look like the diagram.

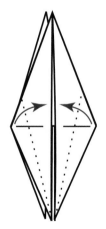

10. Fold sides in to meet in center. Repeat on other side.

11. Crease bottom flaps, both sides.

12. Invert folds and bring bottom flaps up. Your paper should look like the diagram. Invert fold on one flap to make head.

13. Spread out wings and shape crane.

Crane Ornament

MATERIALS: 6" square of Lavender Washi paper • 18" of ⅛" Pink sheer ribbon • 8 Lavender and 3 Green glass beads • 10" of 24 Gauge Copper wire • Round-nose pliers • Blunt needle
INSTRUCTIONS: Fold crane following diagrams. Thread ribbon in needle. Tie knot, add 4 Lavender beads, tie knot and pierce crane with needle. Repeat on other side of crane. Pierce crane with wire. Add Green beads and spiral wire to secure beads.

Cranes

MATERIALS: 6" squares of Washi paper (Pink, Green, Peach, Black) • 36" of ⅛" Pink sheer ribbon • 15 Pink glass beads • Blunt needle
INSTRUCTIONS: Fold cranes following diagrams. Thread ribbon in needle. Leaving 11" tail, tie knot and pierce crane with needle. Thread cranes on ribbon adding beads between cranes and tying knots on each side of cranes to secure.

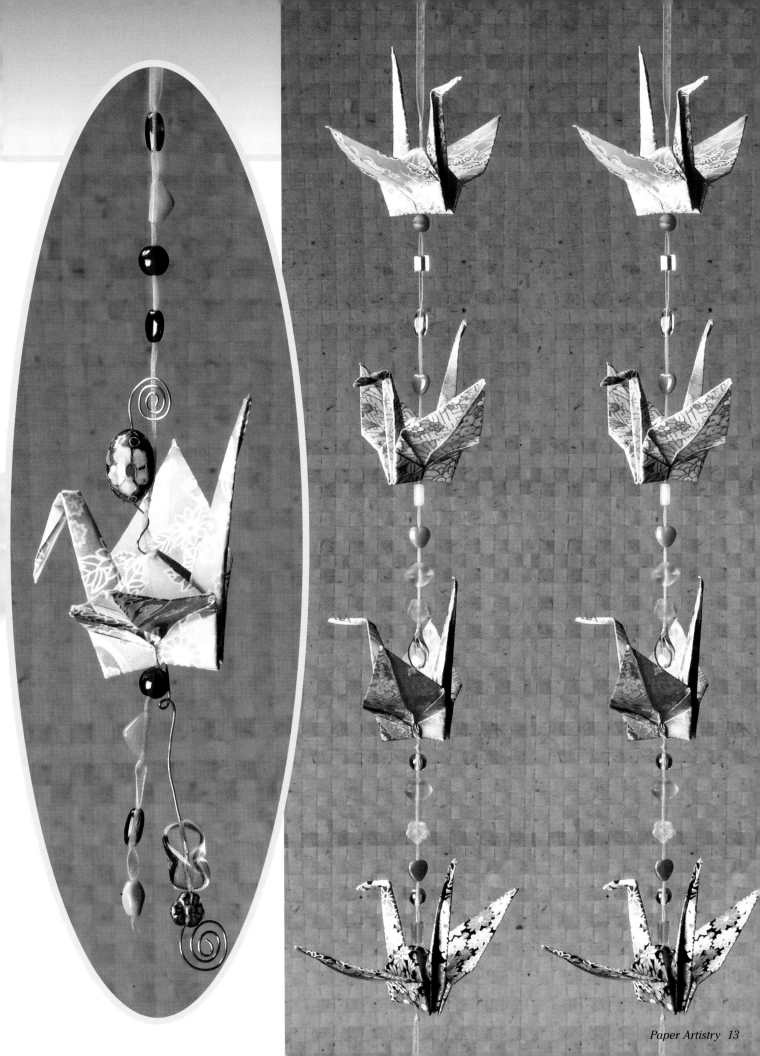

Cherry Blossom Bowls

by Kathy Yoshida

A perfect complement to your Asian themed party… flower-shaped dishes filled with goodies.

Cherry Blossom Bowls

MATERIALS FOR LARGE BOWL: Five 6" squares of pastel printed decorative paper • Glue

MATERIALS FOR SMALL BOWLS: Five each of 3" squares of paper (Pink print, Blue print, Lavender print) • Glue

INSTRUCTIONS: Fold paper squares following diagrams. Glue sections together to form bowl.

Blossom Folds

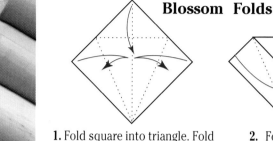

1. Fold square into triangle. Fold 2 outer edges in aligning them with center. Fold top down.

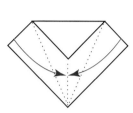

2. Fold 2 outer edges in.

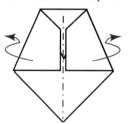

3. Fold back in half.

4. Fold top triangle down to crease. Fold bottom triangle up crease.

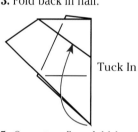

Tuck In

5. Open top flap, fold bottom triangle up and tuck under top triangle.

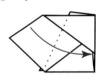

6. Fold flap back to right.

7. Fold top triangle in, Fold bottom of front and back flaps up to form crease.

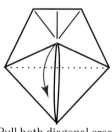

8. Pull both diagonal creases out to unfold. Fold top of triangle down.

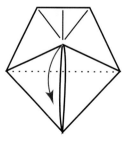

9. Fold along creases as shown, bringing top center forward.

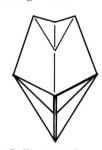

10. Pull out at the center front to create cup. Attach five pieces together to make bowl.

Fashion Folders

Fold bright patterned papers into holders for anything from postage stamps, to business cards, to monetary gifts.

by Karen Thomas

Holder Folds

Money Holder - 8½" x 11" sheet of double sided paper
Card Holder - 12" x 14" sheet of double sided paper
Stamp Holder - 6" square of double sided paper

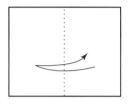 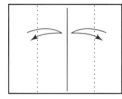

1. Fold paper in half, unfold.　　**2.** Fold edges to center, unfold.

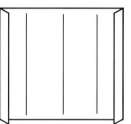 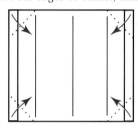

3. Fold ¾" hem on sides, crease well.　　**4.** Fold all corners to first folded edge.

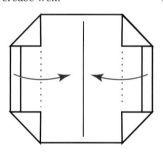 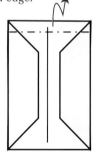

5. Fold in to center on existing fold line.　　**6.** Fold edge back 1". Turn over.

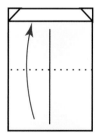 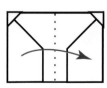

8. Your paper should look like the diagram.

7. Fold in half and tuck into corner flaps. Crease well.

9. For money holder, fold short sides together then follow card case folding steps.

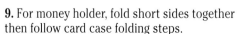

Holders　　*Origami model created by Humiaki Huzita*

MATERIALS FOR MONEY HOLDER: 12" x 14" piece of Black/Red double sided heavyweight decorative paper
MATERIALS FOR CARD HOLDERS: 8½" x 11" piece of Black/Red double sided or Red heavyweight decorative paper • 4" x 5¼" piece of Washi paper for

liner • Asian character rubber stamp • Black ink pad
MATERIALS FOR STAMP HOLDER: 6" square of Black/Red double sided heavyweight decorative paper • 2¾" square of Turquoise paper for liner
INSTRUCTIONS: Fold holders following the diagrams. Insert liner paper if you desire.

Christmas Tree

Fold Christmas accents that are sure to please. Use them as ornaments or as embellishments for greeting cards.

Christmas Tree Folds

by Kathy Yoshida

6" square of paper

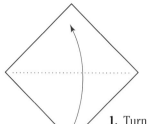

1. Turn square and fold into triangle.

2. Fold triangle in half.

3. Flatten each pocket to make square.

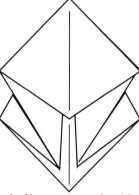

4. Your paper should look like the diagram.

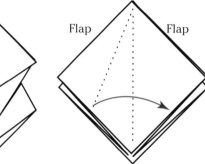

Flap   Flap

5. Crease in center to make flaps.

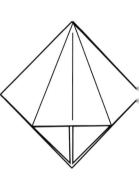

6. Flatten each flap down.

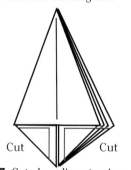

Cut   Cut

7. Cut along lines to give tree shape.

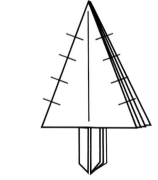

8. Make ¼" slits along edge of tree.

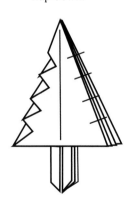

9. Fold down along each slit.

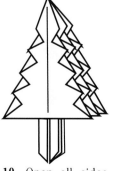

10. Open all sides to make tree.

Trees   *Origami model created by Kazuo Kobayashi*
MATERIALS FOR SILVER TREE: 6" square of Silver/Red paper
• 2 Silver beads • 24 gauge Red wire • Round-nose pliers
MATERIALS FOR GREEN TREE: 6" square of Green/Silver paper
• Scrap of Red cardstock • ½" star punch • 4 Gold and 4 Red eyelets • Eyelet setter • Hammer • Glue
INSTRUCTIONS: Fold trees following diagrams. Punch and glue star to top of Green tree. Set eyelets down edges of tree following manufacturer's instructions. For Silver tree, run 10" of wire through center, add beads on ends and make spirals to secure beads. Glue trees on cards if desired.

Folded Church

Folded churches bring serene beauty to your baptism, christening, first communion or Christmas cards.

Church Folds

6" square of paper

by Kathy Yoshida

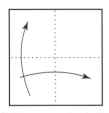

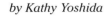

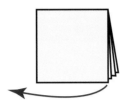

1. Fold square in half to form rectangle and then in half again to form square.

2. Open top pocket to form triangle

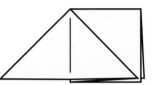

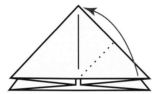

3. Open pocket, flatten and create triangle. Repeat on the other side.

4. Crease as shown. Fold up top right flap.

5. Crease again as shown.

6. Pull down left side of crease to form square. Flatten.

7. Form crease at top left of square as shown.

8. Pull left edge of crease across to right to form a triangle. Flatten

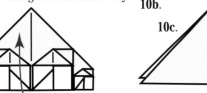

10a. Complete left side of triangle in the same way.

10b.

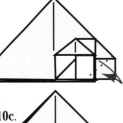

10c.

9. Crease back angle of triangle as shown and follow steps 5 through 8 to complete right side.

11. Lift triangle up and add a cross.

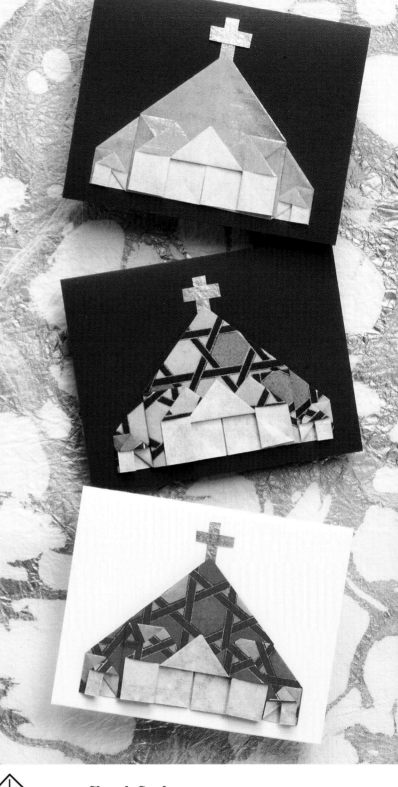

Church Cards

MATERIALS FOR GOLD CARD: 6" Square of Gold Washi paper • 5½" x 8½" Piece of Dark Blue cardstock • ¼" x ¾" and ¼" x 1" Strips of Metallic Gold paper • Glue

MATERIALS FOR BLUE CARD: 6" Square of Blue/Gold print Washi paper • 5½" x 8½" Piece of Dark Blue cardstock • ¼" x ¾" and ¼" x 1" Strips of Metallic Gold paper • Glue

MATERIALS FOR RED CARD: 6" square of Red/Gold print Washi paper • 5½" x 8½" piece of White cardstock • ¼" x ¾" and ¼" x 1" strips of Metallic Gold paper • Glue

INSTRUCTIONS: Fold cardstock in half for card. Fold church following diagrams. Glue paper strips for cross and church on card.

Wonderful Pocket Books

These darling little pocket books are so cute. They make a nice presentation for money gifts. Use the other pockets for poems or little notes.

Folded Pocket Books
inspired by Linda Elliot

MATERIALS: 10¼" x 3¼" Piece heavy cardstock • Various Origami paper scraps • Assorted fibers, Gold cords, beads, Mizuhiki paper cords • Scissors • Glue

INSTRUCTIONS: Glue paper to cardstock. For book cover, fold 2⅜" flap over and glue down. Following the diagram, score and fold along remaining cover lines. Refer to the pictures for embellishments. Fold the pockets following diagrams. The folding allows pockets to stay together without using glue or stitching. Glue end panels of pockets to inside covers of book. The finished book will have pockets that open for inserting photos or mementos.

See Josephine Knot. on page 3.

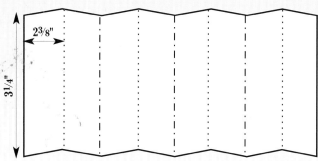

1. Score and fold paper strip into equal sections.

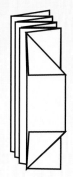

2. With fan closed, fold both corners of first section down at a 45* angle.

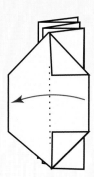

3. Continue opening fan and folding corners of each section, creasing folds well.

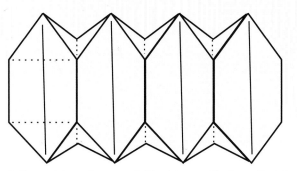

4. Open strip and reverse folds at top and bottom. Push in with fingers while folding back along previous creases.

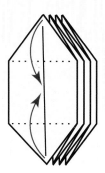

5. Close unit and place on table vertically so pages open like a book.

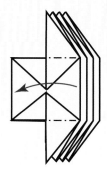

6. On each page fold tip and bottom corners down along center fold line.

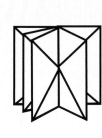

7. Finished fold. Turn over for pocket book

Not only are these little pocket books aesthetically pleasing to the eye, they are functional too! This is a great way to give a gift of money with a special note inside. Use the books for storing inspirational and motivational notes; that way they are always at your fingertips.

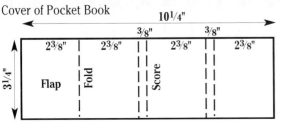

Cover of Pocket Book

23/8"	23/8"	3/8"			23/8"	3/8"		23/8"
Flap	Fold		Score					

10 1/4"

3 1/4"

Flower Star Books

1. Fold 4" square in half on the diagonal to form triangle. Unfold

2. Valley fold up, fold the other 2 corners together on the diagonal. Unfold.

3. With valley fold side up, fold in half.

4. Place on table with folded edge at the top.

6. Unfold entire square. Reverse folds to make the pattern between the diagonal valley folds to be: peak, valley, peak.

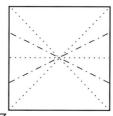

5. From center point, fold right side of folded edge down to meet mountain fold. Repeat on left side.

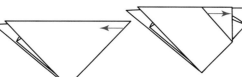

7. Fold and collapse into a triangle. Place on table with open side of triangle at the top.

8. Fold the right corner of the top layer to the center and crease. Fold that tip back to the fold you just made.

9. Repeat step 8 on remaining corners. Unfold all corners and reverse fold the 2 folds in each corner. Push in the first fold and pull out the second fold. Repeat on 3 other corners.

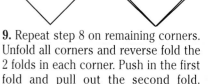

10. Fold small triangles on both sides up and over the front. Unfold and reverse fold. Push to inside.

Flower Star Book
by Sheila Cunningham

Flower Star Book Pattern

MATERIALS: Vellum • Decorative paper • Matboard • Art knife • ⅛" Satin ribbon • Glue
TO MAKE BOOK : Make 5 sections using basic fold. Glue flat side of one section to flat side of next section with points together and all open ends facing same direction. Trace and cut out 2 cover patterns. Cover with decorative paper allowing ¼" all around to fold under. Match the halfway point of 27" ribbon to bottom point of inside cover, glue ribbon from this point to center of top. Glue block of 5 sections on top of this. Place ribbon over bottom points of the 5 sections up to center of top edge, glue. Glue second cover on top of this. Tie book open to see flower formation.

Pleated Star Books

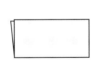

1. Fold 4" vellum square in half.

2. Fold in half again.

3. Unfold and turn over.

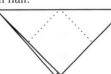

4. Fold on the diagonal, folded edge at top.

5. From center top folds, fold top edge down to meet the valley fold and crease.

6. Fold new edge back to the edge you just creased.

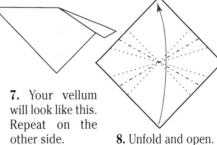

9. Place as shown, valley folds facing up. Make sure folds between horizontal and vertical valley folds are correct. Reverse folds to fit this pattern. Fold pleats, collapse into a square. Pleat points will extend beyond the square.

7. Your vellum will look like this. Repeat on the other side.

8. Unfold and open.

Pleated Points Star Book

Created by Sheila Cunningham

MATERIALS: Two 2¼" x 2¼" matboard • Five 4" squares of vellum • Decorative paper • 27" of ⅛" Satin ribbon (For White & Gold book use ³⁄₁₆" sheer ribbon) • Art knife • Glue

TO MAKE BOOK: Make 5 sections using basic fold. Glue sections together matching up bottom points with all open ends facing same direction. Cover matboard with decorative paper. Place on table with inside of cover facing up. Match center point of the ribbon to 1 corner, glue ribbon from this point to opposite corner. Glue block of 5 sections on top of this. Make sure the bottom point and the opposite point on the open end are glued on the ribbon. Place ribbon over bottom points of the 5 sections up to the opposite corner, glue. Glue second cover on top of this. Pleated points on either side of book will extend beyond cover. Tie book open to see pleated points star formation.

Vellum Christmas Ornaments

Vellum Christmas Ornament or Suncatcher

by Catherine Mace

MATERIALS: 5 squares pastel vellum • Glue stick • 18" gold cording • Small glass pearls • White craft glue • Small hole punch • Optional: Crystal glitter and Gold pen

INSTRUCTIONS: Fold each square, referring to folding diagrams. Attach each folded section to the next with the glue stick, very lightly but completely coating the small square of paper that results from the folding. Glue 1st section to last section so starburst shape is formed. Punch small hole in area where 2 sections are glued together. Thread gold cord through hole and tie knot at both ends. If desired, use white craft glue to attach pearl to center of starburst and sprinkle with crystal glitter.

NOTE: Large snowflake ornament uses five 4"squares. Regular ornaments use five 2" squares. Small gold ornament uses five 1" squares.

Use versatile vellum to create suncatchers and beautiful Christmas ornaments. Rubber stamp and trim with jewels and glitter. Create a small book with a message inside to send out a holiday greeting that transforms into a Christmas ornament for the recipient!

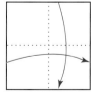

1. Fold paper in half in both directions to form a cross.

2. Unfold and turn the paper over. Fold diagonally to form triangle.

3. Your paper will look like this.

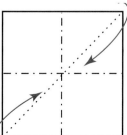

4. Unfold. Collapse the fold by pushing the diagonal to form a small square.

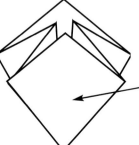

5. Your paper will look like this.

6. Glue these surfaces together to form a suncatcher.

Christmas Message Folding Book Ornament

by Catherine Mace

MATERIALS: White copy paper, cut into 4" squares or larger • Assorted *Hero Arts* holiday rubber stamps • Metallic Gold & Green inks • Sponge• Glue stick • Cardstock • Beads • Thin gold cording

INSTRUCTIONS: Before cutting copy paper into squares, first use printer or rubber stamps to print out holiday messages. Cut out 4 or 5 squares of paper so printed message is centered on each square. Use sponge and inks to add color to paper squares. Stamp small holidays images on paper. Fold each square, according to folding diagram. Glue each folded square back to back with other squares with glue stick but do not glue 1st square to last square, as in suncatchers. Cut cardstock same size or slightly larger than folded square and cover with decorative paper. Glue thin gold cording to 1st and last squares, then glue cardstock covers on top of cording to act as book covers. Thread glass beads onto cording.

Padded Paper Books

by Michelle Ross

Padded paper refers to a stack of papers glued together at one edge to make a writing pad, a process easily done by hand.

These books make wonderful gifts for those really special people in your lives. Start your book today!

Purple & Gold Padded Paper Book

MATERIALS: Two 4" x 4" bookboards • ½" x 4" bookboard spine piece • One each 9¼" x 5", 8½" x 3⅞", 1⅝" x 3⅞" Purple/Gold Yuzen paper • 60 Sheets of 3⅞" x 3⅞" padded paper (see directions above) • Metallic Gold pen • Small White domino game pieces • Permanent Black ink • Assorted rubber stamps • Mauve pigment ink • Clear embossing ink • Clear powder • Gold embossing powder • Heat tool • Scraps Gold and Black velvet or suede paper • Skeleton leaf • White glue
INSTRUCTIONS: Construct book as described above. Use Gold pen to gild page edges while still clamped together. Stamp game pieces with Asian images and Black ink, let dry. Color pieces with Mauve ink, emboss with clear powder. Glue Black and Gold velvet paper to cover, glue on skeleton leaf and game pieces.
TIP: If Gold skeleton leaf is not available, drag embossing pad over plain skeleton leaf, sprinkle with Gold embossing powder, and heat to melt.

Burgundy & Gold Padded Paper Book with Matching Pencil

MATERIALS: Two 4" x 5⅝" bookboards • ½" x 5⅝" bookboard spine • 3¼" x 5½" Padded paper (see directions above) • Burgundy/Gold Yuzen paper (6½" x 9½" - outside cover; 8⅝" x 5½" - inside cover; 1⅝" x 5½" - pad spine cover; 4" x 3" - pencil loop; 1½" x 4¼" - pencil) • 5½" Round pencil, sharpened • White shrink plastic • Assorted rubber stamps • Quick-drying pigment inks • Red & Gold paper scraps • Bone folder • Glue stick • Tacky White glue
INSTRUCTIONS: See directions above for Red Padded Paper Book. To cover pencil, cut paper approximately 1½" x 4¼", to reach from metal ferrule below eraser to top of painted wood. Completely coat wrong side with thin coat of tacky glue, allow to set up for 1 minute. Lay pencil on strip, carefully roll up. Smooth sides of pencil with bone folder, removing excess glue and air bubbles. Set aside to dry. To make loop, fold each side of 4" edge of paper to wrong side center, 2" x 3" doubled thickness, glue down. Fold strip around pencil to determine loop size needed. Glue loose ends together, with pencil in place. When dry, glue loop ends under pad, glue pad to inside back cover. Cut shrink plastic approximately 1" x 1¾", gently round corners with scissors. Stamp images with Burgundy ink, add various background and text images in other colors. Rub pigment colors onto plastic. Shrink with heat tool or oven. Cut graduated sizes of rectangles of Red, Gold, and patterned papers. Place and glue them slightly twisting each piece as pictured. Use tacky glue to attach plastic decoration. Do not sharpen paper-covered pencils in electric sharpeners, they will jam the mechanism.

Red Padded Paper Book

MATERIALS: Two 4" x 5⅝" bookboards • ½" x 5⅝" Bookboard spine piece • 60 Pieces text paper 3⅞" x 5½" • Decorative paper (6½" x 9½" - outside cover; 8⅝" x 5½" - inside liner; 1⅝" x 5½" - spine cover) • Two 1" x 5⅝" strips masking tape • Decorative edge scissors (optional) • Glue stick • Bone folder • White glue • Waxed paper • 2 Clamps • 1" x 5" Muslin • Paper clay • Terra cotta pigment ink • Waxy Gold rub-on color • Graphic Ladies rubber stamp by *Y.I. Stamp, Ink!* • Scrap Black velvet or suede paper • Scrap of Gold tissue
PAD INSTRUCTIONS: Select edge to glue. Fan pages, apply White glue to fanned edges. Fan in other direction, apply more adhesive to same edge. Straighten stack of paper, cover glued area with waxed paper to prevent clamps from sticking. Clamp to hold while drying. Glue muslin strip across glued spine edge. Wrap and glue decorative paper pad spine cover over muslin. Alternately, have a print or copy shop pad and trim your paper.
INSTRUCTIONS: Lay out bookboards and spine so space between each board is twice the thickness of one board, tape together. Coat back of this assembly with glue stick. Glue unit to 6¼" x 9½" decorative paper. Smooth paper with bone folder to remove air bubbles. Miter corners, glue flaps to inside. Glue 8⅝" x 5½" decorative paper liner inside, starting in center. Use bone folder to adhere well and form and mold "gutter" of book, the center inside spine. Glue previously prepared pad of paper to inside back cover of book. To make front cover embellishment, roll paper clay ⅛" thick. Cut to a rectangle 1⅞" x 3¼". Press rubber stamp into paper clay, allow to dry. Color with pigment ink and Gold rub-on color. Tear or cut strips of Gold tissue, apply to cover, top to bottom, and to edge of spine with adhesive. Glue rectangle of velvet paper and embellishment to cover.

Skinny Books

Whether you choose to have printed paper pages or blank pages for adding little quotes or affirmations, these skinny books are wonderful!

Red Palm Leaf Book
by Lea Cioci

MATERIALS: Two 2" x 8" bookboards • Two 2½ x 9½" pieces Red Indian silk-screen paper • Four 2" x 8" strips Tan cardstock • Two 2" x 8" pieces Gold metallic paper • Glue stick • Gold eyelets and eyelet setter • Awl or screw punch • 20" Fibers or cord • Beads • Black pigment ink • *Hero Arts* Woman and floral rubber stamps

INSTRUCTIONS: Cover each bookboard with Red paper, mitering corners and using glue stick. Use Gold metallic paper to line inside of boards. Punch hole ¼" in from both ends. Attach eyelets to outside of covers. Punch holes in each page, using cover as template to determine placement. Tie knot 3" from one end of fiber or cord. Add 2 beads and knot, leaving cord end. Stack covers and pages, thread cord through holes, pulling beads tightly against bottom of book. Bring cord across top of book, down through holes to bottom of book. Tie a knot 3" from end of cord, add 2 beads, knot end. Use cord to wrap around the book several times, use bead tucked through cord wrappings to close the book.

Purple Palm Leaf Book
by Lea Cioci

MATERIALS: Two 1½" x 6" bookboards • Two 2" x 7" pieces Purple Indian silk-screen paper • Four 1½" x 6" strips assorted cardstock • Two 1½" x 6" strips Lilac bamboo impression paper • Glue stick • Gold eyelets and eyelet setter • Awl or screw punch • 15" Colored yarn • Beads

INSTRUCTIONS: Follow instructions for Red Palm Leaf Book. Leave pages blank to show off the interesting textures and colors of the paper.

Nested Boxes

by Lauren Johnston

Large Box Pattern

Fold & Score along dotted lines.

These beautiful boxes are easy to make. Use sheets of decorative paper for the coverings. You can make earrings to match the boxes.

Red Nested Boxes

MATERIALS: Large sheets coordinating designs Red Indian silk-screened paper • Gold cardstock • Craft knife or scissors • Metal-edged ruler • Fine-tipped permanent pen • Scoring tool • Metallic Gold paint or Gold leafing pen • Adhesive film, adhesive spray or glue stick • Tacky White glue

INSTRUCTIONS: Adhere paper to Gold cardstock using spray adhesive or cold laminating/adhesive machine. Use pattern actual size for largest box. Reduce to 92% for smaller size, further reduce to 85% for smallest box. Cut out, trace patterns onto Gold cardstock side of adhered papers with fine tipped pen. Cut out, score on dotted lines, fold. Using tacky glue, adhere tab on long side of box to inside. For decorative accents on largest box, use scraps of Red paper with Gold backing. Cut 2 pieces, each slightly smaller than the last one for two sides of box. Outline each edge of decorative strips with Gold pen. Glue 2 strips together, glue to sides of box.

Wonderfully Fun!...
Two Gifts in One!

What a fun project to make and even more fun to open as a gift. Not only do you receive a gift inside, you have an ornamental box to pass along the next time you give a gift.

Purple Triangular Nested Boxes
by Lauren Johnston

MATERIALS: Large sheets of Purple Indian silk-screened paper with coordinating designs • Gold cardstock • Craft knife or scissors • Metal-edged ruler • Fine-tipped permanent pen • Scoring tool • Metallic Gold pen • Black foam mounting squares • White glue • Adhesive film • Spray or glue stick

INSTRUCTIONS: Access to copy machine is necessary for this series of nested boxes. For largest box top, copy pattern at 100%, for box bottom reduce to 97%. For medium box top, 92% and medium box bottom, 89%. For smallest box top, 84% and bottom at 81%. Adhere purple paper to gold cardstock, wrong sides together, using spray adhesive or cold laminating/adhesive machine. Trace patterns onto gold cardstock side with fine-tipped permanent pen. Cut out all boxes on solid lines. Score on dotted lines. Apply glue to triangular tabs at each box corner. fold tabs in, hold in place until glue dries. Repeat, making 3 boxes. For top decoration of largest box, make 4 triangle shapes from paper scraps mounted on cardstock, largest is 3½" each side, smallest is 1⅛". Outline each triangle shape with gold, edge each box with gold. Stack gilded triangles, secure with mounting squares.

Earring Pattern Cut2

Cut Here

Large Box Pattern

Score & fold along dotted lines.

Cut Here

Purple Heart Charm Earrings

MATERIALS: Clear shrink plastic • Fine-tipped permanent pen • Purple paper scraps • Tacky White glue • Clear bonding glue • Gold jump rings • 2 Gold heart charms • Flat earring backs • ⅛" Hole punch • Pushpin

INSTRUCTIONS: Trace triangle pattern onto clear shrink plastic. Cut out with scissors, cut away ink marks. Use hole punch to make hole near 1 point. Shrink plastic in oven or with heat tool. Cut piece of Purple paper slightly larger than shrunken plastic. Coat 1 side of earring triangle with White glue, apply Purple paper, right side facing into plastic. When glue dries, pattern will be visible through plastic. When dry, trim off excess paper. Use pushpin to make hole in paper over punched hole. Paint edges of plastic Gold. Attach charm with jump ring through hole. Use bonding glue to attach earring back to paper side of triangle, with charm hanging below bottom point.

Heart Charm Earrings

by Lauren Johnston

Are you a box or container freak? Well, these triangular boxes are just what you need for part of your collection. You'll find other boxes and containers scattered throughout Paper Artistry. Make them all to round out your collection!

Fabulous Folios

A folio is simply a folded piece of paper. From that simple form all kinds of imaginative and intriguing projects begin. Get inspired… get started!

Pastel Mirror Book
by Catherine Mace

MATERIALS: Two 2½" x 3½" bookboards • Pastel Yuzen (3¼" x 8"; Two 2¼" x 3¼"; 1½" x 2½" Scrap Yuzen) • 2" x 3" Mirror • 18" Adhesive-backed Copper tape • Acrylic gloss medium and varnish • Paintbrush • Gold colored brass charm • Copper metallic ink pad • Spray sealer • Tacky White glue • Glue stick • Bone folder

INSTRUCTIONS: Center bookboards on long Yuzen strip, leaving ¼" between bookboards for ease. Glue in place, making sure tops and bottoms of boards line up. Trim corners of Yuzen, apply glue to top and bottom flaps, glue down. Use bone folder to smooth out air bubbles. Glue paper spine piece on center-line between boards, it will be glued to the cover and to each board. Use bone folder to make sure piece is well adhered. With glue stick, adhere end papers inside each board. Allow to dry. Paint with 3 coats of gloss medium to protect paper and give a glossy finish. Always paint in same direction, as brush strokes will show. Trim edges of mirror with copper tape, burnish with folding tool and wrap raw edges to back. Use tacky glue to attach mirror to inside of book, let dry. Tap copper ink pad around edges of gold charm; spray to seal. Adhere to cover with tacky glue. Let dry for several hours.

Photo Card
by Catherine Mace

MATERIALS: Two 6¼" x 9" pieces Moss Green Tiziano or other medium weight textured paper • 1 Each 1½" x 6¼" and 2" x 6¼" Italian printed morning glory paper • 2¾" square of cardstock • 3" Square of clear plastic or acetate • 2 photos • Black pen • Craft knife • Cutting mat • Glue stick • Bone folder • White pigment ink • *Paper Parachute* Flowering Vine rubber stamp • White, Yellow, Light Green colored pencils • Metallic Gold pen

INSTRUCTIONS: Fold each piece of Green paper in half to make 6¼" tall cards. Fold narrowest strip of morning glory paper in half, lengthwise. Coat wrong side of strip with glue stick. Lay the 2 Green cards, inside down, on surface, with 6¼" edges almost touching. Lay glued strip on those edges. Smooth with bone folder; trim any excess paper at top and bottom. Fold the joined card in half, right sides of morning glory paper to the inside. Move 3" clear square template around on photo to find best view of picture. Once subject of photo is centered in square, trace around template with pen, cut out. Use cardstock square to determine where to cut opening in card. Photo must be larger than card opening. Tilt squares at an angle to add interest. Trace square on what will become the inside of card. Use craft knife to cut through both thicknesses of Green paper. When card is opened, the 2 openings will mirror each other. Arrange photos behind cut-out squares and tape into place. Fold outside of Green card so 6½" edges almost meet, glue 2nd morning glory strip to those edges. Stamp flowering vine above and below each photo with White pigment ink. Enhance image with White pencil, adding color with Yellow and Green pen-

Continued on page 31.

cils. Decorate front of card with same stamp. Trim with metallic Gold pen. The card will fit into a standard A6 envelope and can be mailed without any additional postage.

Honeycomb Concertina
by Catherine Mace

MATERIALS: Two 2¾" x 3¾" bookboards • Sheet White-on-White Yuzen paper • Chalks • *Postmodern Design* shipping and surcharge stamps • Pale dye inks • Quick drying 3-color metallic color pigment ink pad • Watermark ink pad • Copper, Silver, Gold powdered metallic pigments • Jade and Black quick-drying pearlescent pigment ink • Round sponge • 5" x 25" Black accordion card, scored every 5", or 5" x 25" Black cardstock • Tissues • Straight edge • Pencil • Craft knife • Cutting mat • Black cardstock • Soft-bristled brush • Spray fixative • Metallic Gold thread • Beads • Aluminum coins • Pale Green yarn • Glue stick

INSTRUCTIONS: Sponge printed side of White-on-White Yuzen with pastel dye-based colors. Rub chalks on back to intensify colors that show through paper. Cut paper into two 3¾" x 4¾" rectangles for book covers. Cover bookboards with hand-colored White Yuzen. Let dry. To make accordion card, score and fold Black cardstock every 2½". With wad of tissue and metallic quick-drying pigment ink pad, dab color all over 1 side of Black accordion card, until paper resembles old, rusted, weathered metal. When dry, use craft knife and straight edge to trim off 1½" from long edge of Black accordion card. Fold each scored section of each part of card in half, creating a 10 panel accordion card and strip. Close the larger card and find exact center on 1 end panel. Mark with a pencil line slightly longer than 1½". Use craft knife and straight edge to cut vertical slit through all 10 thicknesses of card. As 2 layers of card are cut through, open card up and cut through next 2 layers, until all panels have slit cut in center. Trying to cut all 10 thicknesses without opening the card makes a messy appearance. Weave narrow strip through larger panels and arrange as shown in photo to create honeycomb effect. Use watermark ink to stamp shipping and surcharge stamps on Black cardstock. Let dry 1 minute, then sprinkle with Silver, Gold and Copper powdered pigments. Brush gently with soft-bristled brush. Blow off excess. Allow to dry, brush off remaining excess. Spray with fixative, cut out. Use glue or double-sided tape to attach symbols to book pages where desired. Apply Jade pigment ink to aluminum coins, then dab with Black pigment ink; heat with heat tool to dry set. Repeat on back side. To mimic appearance of aged patina, it may take 2 applications of inks and 2 heatings to achieve desired effect. Thread beads and coins on lengths of Gold thread. Tie double length of Pale Green yarn around book to keep it closed. Tie beads and coins onto yarn closure.

Small Folded Triangle Pouch

by Catherine Mace

MATERIALS: 1 Sheet each Black and Ivory printed paper • Spray adhesive or other adhesive • L-shaped ruler • Pencil • Scoring tool or bone folder • Scissors • Metallic Gold pen • Red and Gold tassel • Red cinnabar butterfly bead • Tacky White glue • Glue stick

INSTRUCTIONS: Adhere Black sheet to Ivory, wrong sides together. Let dry. Trim to 10¼" x 7½". Referring to diagram, use bone folder and ruler to mark creases on the Ivory side. Measure and make a tiny mark with pencil; then lay straight edge across, score. Accurate measuring and scoring is critical; be sure to take into account width of scoring tool. Don't mark lines with pencil, this is shown only for illustration purposes. Note that when marking along the longer side, all of the measurements are in increments of 2½", except for one, which is only ¼". This will become the hinge for top flap of pouch. With Ivory side up, fold on all dotted lines, all are valley folds. Sharply crease these folds with bone folder. Cut away all unused areas on solid lines, revealing a 7½" square marked in a grid of 2½" squares, with a pointed flap at one end. Turn paper over to Black side. Referring to diagram, mark the diagonal creases shown in Red. Valley fold these creases sharply. These will fold in opposite direction of 1st set. Note upside-down V fold on each side. Turn paper over, Ivory side up; it will be raised in center. Push down middle and each corner will pop up if scoring was done correctly. Push upside-down V sides together, top points touching, collapse all folds to make pouch shape. If scores have been done correctly pouch will come together easily. If any of the folds are off, they can now be recreased to make them fold correctly. The ¼" wide hinge of top flap will cover tops of all folds. Use Gold pen around flap edges, before attaching closure. Snip off 1 Red fringe from Gold tassel; thread remaining cord and tassel through cinnabar bead. Push bead down cord to rest on other Red fringe end. Unravel open end of tassel for about 2". Use Gold threads to tie onto loose Red tassel fringe, tie in knots to secure. Wrap remaining Gold threads around tassel stem, secure with drop of glue. Let dry completely. Use the threads as closure for triangle pouch.

Large and Small Triangle Pouch Dimensions

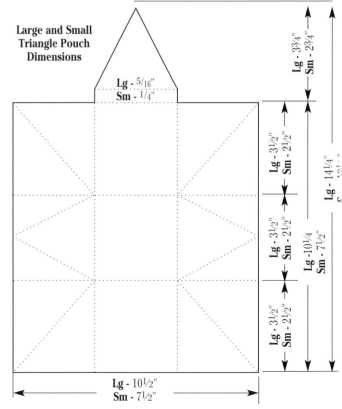

Lg - 5/16"
Sm - 1/4"

Lg - 3¾"
Sm - 2¾"

Lg - 3½"
Sm - 2½"

Lg - 14¼"

Lg - 3½"
Sm - 2½"

Lg - 10¼"
Sm - 7½"

Lg - 3½"
Sm - 2½"

Lg - 10½"
Sm - 7½"

Unique Triangle Pouches

Here is a unique way to wrap up little treasures. The container becomes part of the gift!

Make the larger pouch from printed paper squares adhered to cardstock for strength. Tie the smaller pouch with gold cord threaded through a butterfly bead.

Large Folded Patchwork Pouch
by Catherine Mace

MATERIALS: One 11" x 17" sheet cardstock • 4 Sheets assorted coordinated print paper • 1½" Square punch • Straight edge • Pencil • String or ribbon • One set hook-and loop closure circles • Paper clip • Acrylic spray sealer • Tacky White glue • Glue stick

NOTE: If using directional patterns, pay close attention to where they will appear in completed project so designs don't appear upside down on front.

INSTRUCTIONS: Punch out 12 or 15 squares from each sheet of paper. Use large sheet of cardstock to make triangle pouch as described above, except make each square on grid 3½" x 3½" and allow $5/16$" for hinge of top flap. Score and fold all creases, both sides of paper. Coat back of 1 paper square with glue stick and apply it to cardstock, lining up 1 edge of square with one of the creases that defines the back of pouch. Let squares go over creased edges at least ¼" to insure they will stay in place when pouch is re-folded. Apply additional paper squares, alternating patterns and colors, lining these up with 1st square and crease line. Lay out entire row, adjust colors, if needed, glue in place. Continue until the entire cardstock is covered. Before glue is completely dry, refold on crease lines, to stretch the paper. Reform into pouch shape. Close pouch, wrap with string or ribbon. Allow to dry overnight. Put 1 small drop of White glue on center back of fuzzy piece of hook-and-loop material. Place circle about 1½" up from bottom of flap. Stick other half of closure to glued piece, put 1 drop glue on back of it, close pouch. Use paper clip to keep pouch closed for 2 hours while glue dries. Once dry, if closure is difficult to open, use scissors to trim off a few loops to weaken the bond. Hook-and-loop is often stronger than strength of the paper. If changes, mistakes or dirty spots on finished project are to be altered, punch a new square of paper, glue in place. Spray with 2 coats of sealer to protect paper if container is to be used.

Red, Black and White Bracelet instructions on page 34.

Fashion Bracelet

by Catherine Mace

This dangle bracelet is  snap to make. You'll be prou to say, "I made it myself!"

Red, Black and White Bracelet

MATERIALS: Clear unsanded shrink plastic • Paper scraps • Scissors • Aluminum foil •  x 4" bookboard or thick cardboard • Clear la quer glaze or dimensional adhesive that drie hard & clear • Paintbrush • 6 black "E" beads 3 red oval beads • 12 brushed gold seed bead • 6 gold head pins 1½" long • Red Cinnaba heart beads • 150 gold jump rings • Magnetic gold closures/clasps • Jewelry-ma ing pliers • Small needle-nosed pliers • Toothpick • White tacky glue

INSTRUCTIONS: Cut foil about 12" squar Wrinkle it up then smooth out flat enough t wrap squares of cardboard. This will be used t press hot plastic shapes flat to impart an o glass texture. Make work surface with 3 layer of foil. Cut 10 rectangles from clear shrink pla tic, about 1" x 1½". Use foil-covered board  hold down each small plastic piece as it  being shrunk. Use it to keep plastic from cur ing and sticking to itself. While still hot, use fo covered bookboard to press plastic pieces fla Let cool, set aside. Cut paper scraps into ¼ wide strips. Using a toothpick, coat wrong sic of each strip with glue, wrap around plast piece. Press with fingers to assure all edges a glued down. Let dry thoroughly. Paint wit clear lacquer on one side, let dry. Lacque other side, let dry. Coat each side twice, pain ing both paper and plastic. Let dry overnigh Use hand or electric drill to drill a ³⁄₆₄" ho through paper and plastic at one end  wrapped pieces. Using pliers, put 1 gold jum ring through each hole. On each head pi thread one small brushed gold seed bead. Ad cinnabar heart and 1 more gold bead. Us round-nose pliers to bend excess wire int hanging loop. Make 2 more. With remainin pins, thread 1st a brushed gold bead, sma black bead, red oval bead, followed by anothe black then gold bead. Bend excess wire int hanging loop. Make 2 more sets. For lin bracelet, partially open most jump rings. Ho 3 closed rings together, put 3 opened ring around that 1st group, close them. 2 links i bracelet made. Add 3 more rings to last grou to create a new link. Continue until bracelet  proper length. Bracelet in photo used 120 jum rings and is 7" long. Insert 1 opened end of  jump ring through ring on back of magneti clasp, attach ring to last 3-ring link of bracele Repeat on other end of bracelet attaching t other end of clasp. Referring to the phot attach plastic charms and bead assemblie around bracelet. Make sure all jump rings ar fully closed.